Taking care of your planet

Click!
energy!

BARRON'S

Every morning when I get up, I prepare a large breakfast because I need a lot of energy in order to start the day with strength.

Did you know that food is the energy source for humans and other living beings? We need energy in order to be able to jump, run, swim, play, carry heavy things, and even think!

A very long time ago, people used their energy to feed themselves and to live—that is, they used their own energy to hunt, fish, build a house, make clothing, and so on. But with the passage of time, people began to make tools and instruments to do all these tasks easily and they invented tools such as knives and hammers.

Then people discovered that other sources of energy could be of great use, such as animal power for transportation and working the land. Gradually, they realized that by taking advantage of the different types of energy present on Earth, people could live in increasing comfort.

Where does the energy we need come from? Inside Earth, there are sources of energy that we can use, like coal, oil, and gas. These natural fuels formed underground millions of years ago. They are the energy sources used to run cars and airplanes and for heating, among other things. The problem is that they are not renewable, they take a long time to form, and they are difficult to get to. Because we use them much more quickly than they form, they will run out. In a single year, we use an amount that nature would take years to produce. What a disaster!

These sources of energy also cause a lot of problems, because when we burn them, they produce smoke and gases that damage the environment; that is, they pollute the air that we breathe, harming our health and that of other living beings.

Have you ever seen the black smoke that comes out of a truck when it starts up? Imagine if all the cars on the road gave off smoke. This smoke enters the air that we all breathe! Yuck!

Fortunately, we can use other types of energy that are much cleaner: Solar panels can be used to generate electricity from the heat of the sun. This type of energy does not create pollution and is very cheap to produce. The force of the wind can also be used to create electricity. In some places, there are fields of windmills for generating wind-powered electricity. They look like strange forests of gigantic metal trees!

Unlike oil and coal, these sources are inexhaustible. We call them renewable energies because, although we use them, they never run out. What good luck!

The energy we can obtain from the elements of nature must be converted into a form we can use, such as electricity, which is one of the sources of energy most commonly used in the home. The electricity is generated in special plants and then transported to other places through electrical cables until it finally reaches the electrical outlet. Have you ever counted how many outlets there are in your home in order to be able to plug in all the different machines?

Can you imagine what would happen if the whole world had
no electricity? What would happen in your town if everything
suddenly went dark and the traffic lights, trains, and hospital
machines stopped working? It would be a very serious problem!
And what would happen if the television, refrigerator, oven, and
computer switched off in your home? You wouldn't be able
to preserve the food or cook it. You wouldn't be able to see
anything, either; and how would you warm yourself in winter?
Do you realize how important energy
is in our lives?

Although renewable energies are very clean, they can also generate some problems. So, in order to decrease pollution, we must consume less. In your house and in the street, there are many things you can do to save energy. Do you like browsing the Internet? Get used to turning the computer off when you're not using it; otherwise, it will continue to use energy. And if you need to print something, print on both sides of the paper, because a lot of energy is required to produce paper, glass, and metal.

If we make the most use of sunlight, as the children in this image, which is natural, free, and does not pollute, we will save electrical energy. Many countries practice daylight savings: In spring they put the clocks forward one hour so that days are longer and it gets dark later, so they can make use of natural light.

Besides this, houses that have inside walls and ceilings painted light colors make more use of natural light. You can also use energy-saving lightbulbs, which use much less electricity than traditional lightbulbs and can last up to ten times longer. However, the lightbulb that consumes the least is the one we don't turn on. Get used to turning off the light when you leave a room.

You can also save energy by not using electrical appliances when it is not necessary. Did you know that the refrigerator is the appliance that uses the most? Try to open its door as little as possible. The television is the next highest consumer. It uses electricity when it is plugged in, even though it is switched off. The oven also consumes a lot, and you can save

up to 70 percent of this energy if you use a microwave oven. The washing machine and dishwasher also use a lot of energy, so run them only when they are full. If you can hang the laundry out in the sun to dry, it's much better than using the clothes dryer.

Transportation is the main source of pollution in large cities.
Use public transportation whenever possible. If you must use
the car, ask your parents about carpooling. Four people in one
car is much better than four cars with one person in each one.
Perhaps you can walk or bike to some places.

You may know that there are many objects that run on electricity without being plugged in, such as flashlights, remote-controlled cars, musical toys, and so on. These run on batteries, which are manufactured from metals and chemical compounds that are very harmful to the environment. In order to avoid polluting, it is important not to throw them in the garbage but to take them to a recycling center. In most supermarkets and electronics stores, you will find places where you can dispose of them.

As you have seen, energy is very important.
Without it, our lives would not be so comfortable.
We wouldn't have light or gas or hot water. We must
all try to make the best use of it, without wasting it,
as it is very costly to obtain. We must be careful
not to abuse it to avoid pollution. I already do so.
And you can do so with a simple click.
It's very easy.

Activities

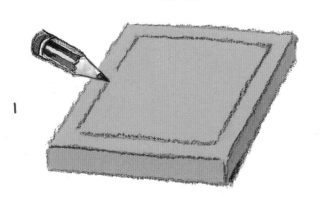

1

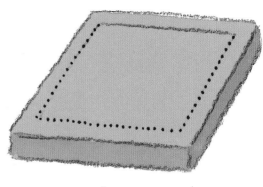

2

Solar oven

Take a pizza box. Using a ruler, draw a fairly large square in the middle of the box, so that each side is 1 inch (2.5 cm) from the edge of the box. Ask an adult to help you cut out three sides of the square, forming a flap. When you have done this, line the flap with aluminum foil (try not to wrinkle it!) and glue it in place. Then, line the inside part of the box with aluminum foil. Cut out a square of plastic laminate almost

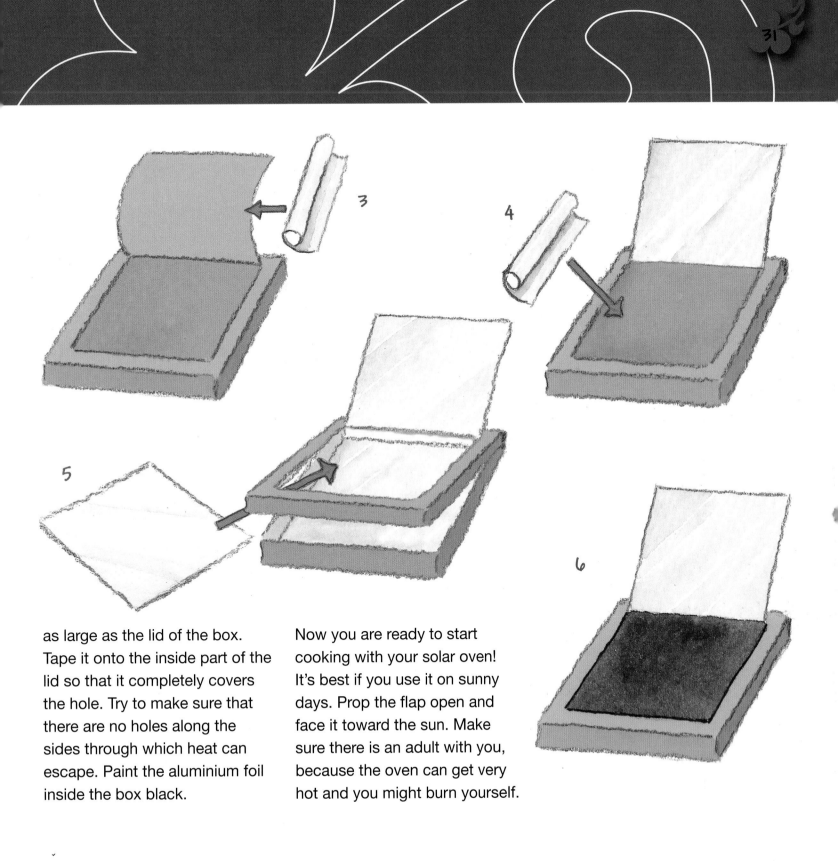

3

4

5

6

as large as the lid of the box. Tape it onto the inside part of the lid so that it completely covers the hole. Try to make sure that there are no holes along the sides through which heat can escape. Paint the aluminium foil inside the box black.

Now you are ready to start cooking with your solar oven! It's best if you use it on sunny days. Prop the flap open and face it toward the sun. Make sure there is an adult with you, because the oven can get very hot and you might burn yourself.

1

2

3

4

A telephone that works without electricity

To make your telephone, get two plastic cups. With a pencil, poke a hole in the bottom of each cup. Tie one end of some string to a paper clip, and thread the other end through the hole in the cup, starting from inside the cup. The paper clip will keep the string from coming through the hole. Then thread the string through the second cup, this time starting from outside the cup. Tie this end of the string to another paper clip. Be sure both paper clips are inside the cups. Now, pull the cups so that the string is tight. One person talks into one cup while the other person listens with the second cup. Communication is assured!

How much energy do you use at home?

Have you ever wondered where the energy you use at home comes from? Does your oven run on gas or electricity? How do you heat the water? Do you have any solar panels on your house? Make a list of the different types of energy you use at home and another list with the things that run on these types of energy. How many things need energy to work? Do you use any systems for saving energy, such as energy-saving lightbulbs or "Energy Star" rated electrical appliances? Can you think of any other ways to save energy?

Parents' guide

What is energy and how do we use it? (pages 2–7)
The concept of energy is abstract and difficult to explain to children. Energy is the capacity to carry out work, such as moving an object or heating a substance. In our daily lives, we use energy continuously: to move about, to obtain heat and light, and so on. Children must understand that having energy is a luxury that is not available to everybody. Energy consumption is closely linked with our lifestyle, and other societies consume much less energy than we do. In a rural community in a less-developed country, for example, almost 90 percent of the energy consumed is used for cooking food, whereas in our homes, this accounts for less than 10 percent.

We can encourage children to think about the daily activities that are essential, such as eating, or going to school, so that they are able to distinguish them from nonessential activities. They can also be encouraged to seek alternatives that imply energy savings: going to school by bicycle instead of by car, for example.

Nonrenewable energies. Fossil fuels (pages 8–11)
Our society is dependent on fossil fuels. However, their use has several negative effects. Every day, millions of tons are extracted, without taking into account that many millions of years were required for their formation. Furthermore, the combustion of fossil fuels produces water and carbon dioxide, one of the gases contributing to the greenhouse effect and oxides of nitrogen and sulfur, which lead to the formation of acid rain. Depending on the children's ages, you can explain this to them. Acid rain is formed when the oxides of nitrogen and sulfur react with the water vapor in the atmosphere to form nitric, nitrous, and sulfuric acids. These acids burn the leaves of the plants and can destroy forests, lakes, and wetlands. With respect to the greenhouse effect, our planet is surrounded by a gaseous layer called the atmosphere, which contains the oxygen we breathe as well as many other gases. The atmosphere enables the sun's light to reach Earth's surface, but it can also trap a considerable part of the heat emitted by Earth. Without this system, Earth would be much colder and we wouldn't be able to survive. If we changed the composition of the atmosphere (for example by releasing more carbon dioxide), too much heat would be retained and the temperature of the planet would rise. This is what we call climate change. The consequences of this remain uncertain, but scientists believe that it could cause

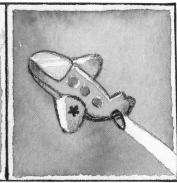

many problems: The polar caps and glaciers would melt, resulting in a rise in sea level, and rainfall could increase in certain regions, resulting in an increase in the incidence of diseases such as malaria.

Renewable energies (pages 12–13)

There are many other sources of energy that we can make use of on our planet that are practically inexhaustible; these are renewable energies. In recent years, renewable energies have become increasingly important because they are cleaner than fossil fuels and are not as potentially dangerous as nuclear energy. These are wind power, wave energy, solar energy, and the heat from Earth itself. In the same group, we include energy originating from biomass, such as firewood.

You can explain to the children that these energy sources are used increasingly, but there is still a lot of room for development and improvement. Only a small part of the energy we consume comes from renewable sources. You can help them understand that the choice of one type or another depends on the region of the planet; for example, in the tropics, it would be an excellent idea to promote solar energy, as tropical areas receive a very high level of solar radiation, whereas in very windy places, it would be very useful to encourage wind power. A combination of these energy sources can also be used. Biomass (from noncultivated trees and organic household waste or agriculture, forests, and livestock) is the main source of energy in some developing countries. However, we must take into account that the uncontrolled use of natural biomass is leading to desertification in many parts of the planet. Furthermore, the use of crops to create biofuels for developed countries can result in a reduction of global food production.

Let's save energy at home (pages18–25)

Children tend to copy adult behavior, so it is important that our habits respect the environment at home. Saving energy does not require great investments. You should simply be consistent when carrying out certain daily tasks, such as switching off (and even unplugging) appliances that are not being used. Between 5 and 15 percent of the energy consumed in the home is used by appliances on stand by. Consumption can also be decreased by using different types of energy-saving lightbulbs, according to the room and usage made of the light, as well as by switching off the lights when they are not necessary. You can also use energy-saving electrical appliances ("Energy Star" rated). With respect to air conditioning, the blinds should be closed in summer during the hottest hours of the day and you should ventilate the house when it is cooler. Another good measure is to regulate the temperature of the thermostat or air conditioner by setting it at 68 to 70° in winter and from 77 to 79° in summer.

The design of the house can also affect energy consumption. If you had to build a new house, you could follow some good advice for making the best use of energy. Compact and rounded forms reduce energy loss. If you live in a cold place, it is best to position the house facing the south and to paint the roof in a dark color. Contrastingly, in very hot places, the facades should be a light color, with few windows facing southward. Insulating the roof can also help to retain the heat in winter and reduce heating in the summer. By installing solar panels, you can generate the electrical energy you need in your home. Finally, painting the walls inside the house with light colors promotes natural luminosity and results in savings in artificial lighting.

Click! energy

Original title of the book in Catalan:
Cuidem el Planeta: Clic! L'Energia
© Copyright Gemser Publications S.L. 2010.
C/ Castell, 38; Teià (08329) Barcelona, Spain (World Rights)
Tel: 93 540 13 53
E-mail: info@mercedesros.com
Website: www.mercedesros.com
Authors: Núria & Empar Jiménez
Illustrator: Rosa Maria Curto

First edition for the United States and Canada published
2010 by Barron's Educational Series, Inc.

All inquiries should be addressed to:
Barron's Educational Series, Inc.
250 Wireless Boulevard
Hauppauge, New York 11788
www.barronseduc.com

ISBN-13: 978-0-7641-4547-6
ISBN-10: 0-7641-4547-9

Library of Congress Control No.: 2009943855

Manufactured by: L. Rex Printing Co. LTD.,
Tin Wan, China
Date of Manufacture: August 2010

Printed in China
9 8 7 6 5 4 3 2 1